Investing

Provide A Guide On How To Maximize Your Profit
Through Short-term Rental Investment

(A Thorough Guide For Young Adults)

Deangelo Fitzpatrick

TABLE OF CONTENT

Investment Funds 1

Enhancing Your Credit Score 33

Real Estate Investment Secrets 60

Not Always Is The Grass Greener 71

Investing Pays 85

Investment Funds 109

You Need Not Take A Vacation 137

Stock Picking 147

Stay Away from Penny Stocks 147

Investment Funds

You are not investing on your own in an asset. There is a pool of investors who contribute money to an aggregate investment.

It is a safer option than purchasing stocks because you are not bearing the risk on your own.

By utilizing an asset, you have access to a greater number of investment opportunities, more administration expertise to assist you, and reduced investment costs than if you were investing on your own.

You do not make individual decisions regarding how the asset's resources should be allocated. You choose an asset based on its objectives, risk, and expenses.

A manager of the asset determines which protections it should hold, in what quantities, and when the protections should be traded. Consequently, you benefit from superior administrative expertise.

You are acquiring shares of this asset. The majority of assets have a specific theme:

- Geographical

- Industrialization

- Varieties of investments

- Size of the firm

There are also numerous types of funds:

- Mutual funds

- Index funds

- Exchange-exchanged funds

- Money market funds

- Hedge funds

The advantages of venture reserves include:

They carry various items.

- Easy to store away

- A professional cashier is required for the shipment.

- Low acquisition cost

The disadvantages are:

• The costs

• Performance or rate of return are not assured.

• You cannot change your investment because the asset manager has control.

You should contribute for a minimum of five years. If you anticipate needing immediate access to your funds, then this may not be the best investment for you.

Utilizing an asset grocery store or stages is the most cost-effective method for depositing funds into reserves. They are available online.

Investing in reserves involves two stages. Initially, you must determine which platform you will use; then, you must decide which project to incorporate.

You will incur fees for both using the platform and purchasing the funds.

Mutual Funds

A shared asset is an asset type. They are investment vehicles that allow you to merge your funds with those of other investors to purchase a variety of stocks, securities, and other investments.

Notably, a financial supporter of a common asset does not possess the protections to which the asset contributes; they only own portions of the asset itself.

You may trade your asset shares once per day at the close of the market for all shared assets. The price fluctuates based on the value of the asset's components at the end of each business day.

You can earn money in three possible ways:

• Income derived from share dividends

• Coupon on bonds

• A rise in the price of protections. If the asset share price is

If the fund grows, you can sell your shares for a profit. There are four types of common funds:

•Those who invest capital in shares (value reserves). They invest in corporate proposals by purchasing shares of a variety of publicly traded companies. They have a greater development potential, but experience cost fluctuations.

• Bonds (fixed-remuneration reserves). The most popular type of fixed pay common assets. Financial supporters are repaid a reasonable amount for their investment in the enterprise. The securities reserve invests in government and corporate debt. They are viewed as a more secure investment than stocks but have less growth potential than value funds. These reserves are frequently well-managed and seek to purchase somewhat undervalued securities to sell for a profit.

• Money market (temporary liability). It consists of secure short-term obligations, typically government Treasury bills. This is a secure location to store your currency. You will not receive substantial returns, but you will not need to worry about losing your initial investment. The average return is somewhat greater than the amount you would obtain from a standard checking or investment account.

•Stocks and bonds. The objective is to reduce risk by investing in both.

diversifying.

•Income reserve. Consistently, they generate current income. These assets are primarily invested in government and high-quality corporate debt, retaining these securities until development generates interest payments. Consequently, they are longer range. However, their primary objective is to generate a steady income for their financial supporters. Common financial supporters are moderate, retired individuals. Charge-aware financial supporters may want to steer clear of these funds because they generate standard pay.

Each common asset is designed to mitigate risk while capturing business sector gains.

The benefits of mutual funds:

• You gain the benefit of having an expert supervisor continuously evaluate your portfolio.

• The cost of the exchange is divided among all investors in the asset, reducing the cost per investor.

- Mutual assets invest in a wide spectrum of areas, immediately differentiating the portfolio.

The obstacles are:

- Costly fees

- Fiscal inefficacy

- inadequate exchange execution

- Possibility of board abuse

Mutual assets may be acquired directly from a shared asset organization, a bank, or a financial institution. Before making a donation, you should create an account.

There are a variety of costs that may be associated with common funds.

Some assets are accompanied by exchange fees or commissions for trading. Annual asset operating expenses are a yearly proportion of the managed assets.

Some assets incur a recovery cost if you sell shares you've only held for a brief duration.

As with any endeavor, there are also risks involved. There is always a possibility that the value of your common asset will decline. Mutual assets are typically more appropriate for long-term investors.

If you anticipate needing your funds shortly, a mutual fund may not be the best choice. This is because the return in that amount of time (after deducting the cost of fees) may not be sufficient to make the investment worthwhile.

Index Funds

A record store is a business that monitors a market file (for example, the S&P 500, the top 500 stocks in the United States).

Typically, they consist of equities or bonds. There is a record and a list reserve for virtually every financial market in existence.

The superintendent of assets constructs a portfolio whose assets reflect the protections of a particular index.

It attempts to replicate the development and execution of a financial market program. It means to match rather than surpass its performance.

It is similar to a shared or trade-exchanged asset.

(ETF). To spend:

Choose the file. There are numerous files that can be followed using file reserves. You can also view area records associated with specific businesses, country files that target equities in single countries, and style files that highlight rapidly growing companies.

• Select a fund

• Buy stocks

The advantages are:

• Broad market openness. There are file archives accessible for a variety of endeavors. Stock record assets and security list funds are available for purchase.

- Low operating expenses. They have a reduced proportion of board costs. The administrator of record subsidizes property exchanges less frequently, resulting in lower exchange fees and commissions.

- Low portfolio liquidity

You can contribute with reduced risk. Most accounts contain dozens or even hundreds of stocks and other investments, and the increase in diversification makes you more resistant to significant losses.

- Since they employ a hands-off approach to investment, they incur lower costs and fees than actively managed reserves. The file store manager must acquire the securities or other interests in a file. He is not required to identify specific performing securities.

• You will incur fewer expenses. In comparison to numerous other investments, they have a high rate of return.

These are the obstacles to a record store speculation:

• You will never outperform the market. They are designed to mirror the performance of the market.

• You have no misfortune protection. When the market plummets, your list asset will plummet as well, as list assets follow their respective business sectors through a variety of difficulties.

- You will not own your favorite stocks eternally.

- No authority over holdings

Generally, the speculation will be conducted over an extended period of time to stimulate positive performance.

Investors make an initial minimum investment ($3,000 - $10,000) and pay annual expenses to maintain the asset (a small proportion of the capital invested).

You can purchase a list reserve directly from a common asset organization or a financial institution. To purchase shares in your preferred list store, you can establish an account directly with the common asset organization offering the fund.

Exchange-Traded Funds (ETFs)

It is a collection of businesses that are sold on a market. Similar to individual equities, ETF shares are traded throughout the day at prices that fluctuate based on supply and demand.

The asset supplier claims the resources, designs an asset to follow their presentation, and then solicits investors for stakes in that asset.

Shareholders own a portion of an ETF, but they do not own the underlying assets.

The primary distinction between ETFs and common assets is that ETF shares trade throughout the trading day, whereas shares of mutual funds only trade once a day after the market closes.

ETFs have become ubiquitous investments. Due to their many benefits, including low cost proportions, liquidity, venture scope, and a low speculation threshold, they are ideal for beginning investors.

Types of exchange-traded funds:

• Bond. It may include government, corporate, and civil securities. Security ETFs detest individual internet-based securities because they lack a maturity date, so their most common use is to produce recurring cash payments to the financial backer. These payments are derived from the interest generated by the individual securities within the fund.

- Businesses. Observe a particular industry

- Products. Invest in commodities such as crude petroleum or gold

The monetary system. Put resources into unfamiliar currencies

A trade-exchanged asset has a price that facilitates its purchase and sale.

You can have an actively managed ETF where portfolio managers are more involved with trading portions of companies; however, an actively managed asset will have higher expenses than an inactively managed asset.

Benefits of ETFs:

- They provide investors with the ability to acquire as stock prices rise and decline

- Investors can benefit from dividend-paying companies.

- Investors in ETFs are eligible for a portion of the earnings

- Flexible. During the day, when business sectors are accessible, ETFs are traded.

- They provide diversification for a portfolio

- Lower price. They are passively due, with significantly reduced cost ratios compared to funds that are actively managed.

- Tax benefits. Due to underlying differences, shared assets incur higher capital charges than ETFs. They have smaller capital additions and are payable upon the ETF's issuance.

Disadvantages of ETFs:

- Subject to display variation

- Subject to administrative expenses and other costs

- The cost could be greater. Assuming that you compare ETFs and investing in a specific stock,

inventory expenses are higher

ETFs are traded through online specialists and traditional representative dealers. You must establish a corporate account.

Money Market Funds

It is a type of common asset that invests in extremely liquid, short-term instruments. They are expected to provide investors with a high degree of dissolvability and an exceedingly low degree of risk.

A venture store company supports the conjecture that is a currency market reserve.

A currency market reserve generates income but minimal capital appreciation, implying that the underlying investment appreciates minimally.

Money market accounts are a wise investment if you can maintain a high minimum balance, limit your withdrawals, and understand that you are not protected against inflation.

They are divided into the following categories:

- Prime liquid assets. Invests non-depository assets in floating-rate obligations and business paper.

The government's currency on hand. Contributes nearly 99.5% of its total assets to actual money and government securities.

- Government reserve. Invest in conventional US depository obligation securities

- Non-taxable cash store. Offer income exempt from U.S. taxation

The benefits of currency market funds are:

- Excellent location to stop currency for the present. Safer due to the fact that these types of assets invest in generally safe vehicles. Consistently generates a low single-digit

return for

investors.

- They invest in extremely fluid security measures. This indicates that financial backers can transfer them easily.

The obstacles are:

- Purchasing power is resilient. They can generate returns under expansion, resulting in diminished purchasing power.

- Fees can consume a substantial portion of the benefit. Usually, a minimum balance is required to avoid a monthly service fee.

- They are not protected by the government. In the event that the investment reserve company becomes bankrupt, you may lose all of your money.

- Low-premium rate

- Inflation danger

Generally, you should pay tax on the premium you receive or the profits generated by the assets as you acquire them. Unless they are held in a tax-exempt retirement account.

In contrast to certificates of deposit, currency market accounts can be closed at any time without penalty.

You can purchase currency market assets from investment firms, financial institutions, and banks.

Hedge Funds

A multifaceted investment is an aggregated speculative reserve that trades relatively fluid resources and can employ more complex trading to improve performance.

A mutual fund's speculation administrator is typically paid an administration fee and a presentation fee.

Investors in speculative stock investments must be qualified (wealthy) monetary supporters.

are believed to be aware of the speculation risks and to acknowledge them because of the potential returns.

The primary goals of speculative stock investments are to maximize returns and reduce risk. They intend to attempt to generate income regardless of the market's direction.

They are frequently readily available to authorized financial supporters. To be considered a certified financial supporter, you must meet one of the following requirements:

- Have an individual pay at least $200,000 for you alone

- You must have personal assets worth more than $1 million

- Must be a superior (chief, chief) involved in diversified investments or have a representative benefit plan or trust fund worth $5 million

The majority of speculative stock investments use a 2 and 20 administrator compensation plan, which provides the mutual fund manager 2% of the assets and a motivational expense of 20%.

Types:

- Macro. Invest in equities, bonds, destinies, alternatives, and occasionally currencies.

- Justice. Attempts to hedge against market value declines by investing in equities or stock files and then selling them.

• Relative value exchange for diverse investments. Purchase protections that are anticipated to increase in value, while selling those that are likely to depreciate.

• Troubled mutual funds. They are frequently associated with credit payments or reorganization.

Hedging reserves invest in real estate, real estate, monetary forms, subordinates, and others. Therefore, they can invest in anything.

The benefits of a support fund are:

• Adaptability. Individuals cannot freely trade mutual funds; as a result, they are more adaptable because there is no centralized body administering their performance.

- Aggressive conjecture technique. This is necessary to achieve a higher return.

- Enhances the likelihood of enhancement. The asset can increase diversification and reduce risk further.

- Guidance from knowledgeable professionals and candor. The flexible investing administrators are also versed in financial administration issues.

These are the disadvantages of speculative stock investments:

- Hedging store costs. Their pricing structure is known as 2 and 20. Financial backers pay a two percent administration fee for the asset's duties. In addition, they pay the asset manager a

20% exhibition fee on any profits earned throughout the year.

• Risks and expected returns. They are considered to be taking so many risks.

• They are typically less volatile than securities or bonds

• You may only be able to withdraw your funds after having contributed for a certain period of time or at certain times of the year.

The minimum initial investment amounts for mutual funds range from $100,000 to over $2 million.

Individual investors have a very difficult time gaining access to high-quality mutual funds, but it is possible to invest in one through a circuitous route. You could invest in the stock of a financial institution that operates fence funds.

Enhancing Your Credit Score

The most straightforward way to improve your financial standing is to consistently pay your obligations on time. As mentioned previously, ensuring that your credit balance is closer to zero than your credit limit will also improve your FICO score. Control who and when your credit is checked with caution. Each time your credit is examined by a potential lender, approximately 10 points are deducted from your score. This may not seem like much, but assuming a few moneylenders check your credit, it could mean the difference between obtaining a reasonable advance and settling for a lower amount or being denied financing altogether.

In addition, when you have paid off all of your credit cards, you will appear to be a wholly dependable borrower, and your credit score will increase significantly.

Each revealing organization has a procedure for you to initiate a debate if you discover errors in your report. Try not to pass up this opportunity. Complete your work and eliminate any irrelevant information.

Again, the quickest way to improve your credit is to pay off your expenses, including your existing credit cards.

Should I invest or pay off my debt?

This is perhaps the most well-known question for first-time financial benefactors. Prior to this juncture, I have discussed the benefits of both options. Similar to the enduring parable about the chicken and the egg, the subject of obligation versus contribution can appear to be a burdensome circumstance to consider. Overall, having fewer obligations will enable you to contribute more, and increasing your contributions will increase your income for meeting obligations. So what is the correct strategy?

Some individuals would advise you to take care of your financial obligations before you begin saving and contributing. This is solid financial advice if you consider the essentials. Why put money in your savings account to earn a few percent if your credit card interest rate is fifteen percent?

Despite the fact that this seems acceptable, it is actually noticeably defective exhortation. I can assure you that if I had waited until all of my expenses were paid off before contributing and investing funds, I would be standing by today. Unless you successfully alter them, the behaviors that led to the debt will persist. You need to pay down your debts to improve your FICO score, but you also need to save money for investments and retail purchases. To state it plainly, there is no straightforward response, much like the chicken and the egg. In the long run, paying off your debt will improve your FICO score, allowing you to purchase a home at a lower interest rate, but in the meantime, it is also prudent to save money for genuine investments. The most important factor is your methodology. Certain individuals must act immediately before the second opportunity disappears. Others can cautiously investigate their path to financial independence. Which path is optimal for you? No one but you can determine.

The importance of cash reserves in real estate investing

When purchasing real estate, you need to have cash reserves. Investing is about risk management. If you begin purchasing real estate without reserves, you assume a greater risk than someone who has reserves. Real estate investing is not without its challenges. What should you do if you get a terrible tenant who destroys your property and does not pay rent? Plan for the worst and hope for the best, even though this is not typical.

I recognize that it is unquestionably difficult to have holds when you are just commencing. In any case, you should have a Plan B in place, even if it involves obtaining additional Visas, placing them in water, and storing them in a container. In the event that something terrible occurs, you will need to melt the ice and endure the downtime. Additionally, while the ice is melting, you will have a few hours to ensure that you need to use the card.

And remember, if you get a second Visa and don't use it, the available unused credit will help boost your credit score.

In actuality, you should cease impulse buying and maintain your stockpiles. There will be many up periods to compensate for these down periods, assuming you have the resources to endure them.

Knowledge Is Strength

Many individuals who invest in land require your financial assistance. Only one in every unusual arrangement is a good one, and there are numerous liars who would love nothing more than to sell you their concerns. Before purchasing your first and every subsequent property, you should conduct your research thoroughly.

How would you implement due diligence? You must read this book and others like it in order to know precisely what to look for. As you gain experience and establish a reputation, opportunities will begin to present themselves. Only one out of every unusual arrangement is a good arrangement, so you need the data to quickly distinguish the bad ones from the good ones.

I am only interested in five or ten out of every twenty homes that I inspect, whether personally or financially. After further investigation, I might make offers on approximately fifty percent of these, and then close on a couple. This represents a ratio of one arrangement per ten possibilities. This does not include properties on the MLS that are generally considered to be market value bargains. You will be successful in real estate investing if you have the knowledge to quickly recognize deceptive advertising, budget summaries, and renovations that conceal hidden problems.

Even if you don't have the funds to purchase your first investment property, you should start working speculative situations and researching properties. By completing the calculations outlined in Chapters 4 and 5, you will become an expert on the local housing market. When a truly advantageous offer is presented to you, you are able to recall it swiftly and act appropriately. If the first deal you examine appears to be too excellent to be true, it is likely that it is. Employ your senses and rely on the numbers! Never make a purchase based on emotion. I've inspected and then rejected a large number of attractive homes that were financial failures. There are numerous exceptional deals available, and you will find them if you are patient and disciplined.

If you adhere to the principles in this book, you will soon be bragging to your companions about your most recent land purchase and the enormous return on investment (ROI) you are receiving. The majority of them will not accept you until you relocate into a nicer residence and quit your job, but you will eventually be accepted. It requires a great deal of effort up front, but when the skills are mastered, the outcome is immense... Once there, there will be no need to turn back!

Excellence Is Not the Name of the Game Anymore

Many individuals argue that doing everything yourself is the best method to maintain the quality of your property. I do not disagree, but when you begin to think in these terms, you begin to teeter on the verge of developing an emotional attachment to your home. You should never have a personal stake in your investment properties. I am aware that this is quite challenging; I have occasionally been at fault for it myself.

Actually, few out of every unusual property should be maintained to the same degree as your own residence. Possibly, on the off chance that you offer premium accommodations. However, the majority of rental properties are not that attractive. In the past, I've worked with deals that were located in areas where it was impossible to attract high-quality tenants, so it would have been a waste to furnish the property with premium materials. You wouldn't have the option to charge more rent for the property since market values only allow you to go so high, so it seems reasonable to match the standard of materials to the property's location and tenant quality. This in no way justifies slumlording, but it does not seem appropriate to maintain

C- or B-grade properties at A-grade quality.

I am familiar with myself. If I were the proprietor of my investment properties, I would be particular about maintaining them to my usual standard. In other words, I would maintain every one of my properties in pristine condition, regardless of whether or not it was practical to do so. By employing a property manager and delegating all authority to him, I don't have to worry about the materials or the property not being in A-grade condition at all times because I don't need to visit the properties. The properties are still kept in immaculate condition, but I don't have to stress about rental-grade versus luxury-grade protection and which I believe is superior.

How much time and mental acuity would it take to maintain a property to your specifications? Contrast this with the amount of compensation you would receive for doing so. As far as I'm concerned, even though I'd adore for all of my properties to be at the highest level possible, the amount of time and effort it would take to get them there does not warrant my concern. Furthermore, it's not a one-time effort; it's one thing to get them to such a high standard, but it's another thing to maintain them there.

Having a property manager manage my properties relieves me of the need to incessantly monitor the properties from a "carefully concealed, out of mind" perspective. For some, the prospect of not seeing their properties and not having the option to assess their condition may send them into a tailspin, but for me, it makes everything simpler and less stressful to not be concerned.

You Will Need to Have Faith in Others

When you delegate labor to others, you must have faith in those individuals. The less work you do, the more work someone else must complete for you; therefore, the more people you should trust. Many individuals struggle to trust others because they lack trust in them. Assuming that you will lose sleep if you entrust others with your property or your business, you should plan to handle everything yourself.

Those of us who are comfortable trusting others cannot assume that things will always go smoothly or that the people we trust today will not likely become dishonest in the future. You must weigh the advantages and disadvantages of entrusting others with your responsibilities, recognizing that they may occasionally falter or take advantage of you, versus performing all of the work yourself. I've gotten into trouble once, twice, or possibly three times by relying on others. This is a reality that you must face. But I'd still choose to be taken advantage of a few times over the hassle of doing all the work myself.

Consider adopting an entrepreneurial stance.

This generates a larger concept, which is commerce. Suppose you intend to launch a business. People have urged you to start a pizza business because you create the world's finest pizzas. This business has two options for pursuing the fundamental structure.

Option one: You are the person responsible for preparing pizzas. If you take time off, pizzas will not be made. In this method, you make no pay. Your genuine presence has a direct effect on earnings.

Option two: You develop frameworks and procedures for your pizza business so that anyone can replicate your pizza. This allows you to remove yourself from the situation and add additional representatives in your stead. When you take a vacation, your business is not affected in any way. Generally speaking, this is how businesses operate. To earn money, pizza makers and burger flippers are not required to perform the actual labor.

You can do all the task yourself or hire others to do it. How you decide to contribute to your land is dependent on the prior discussion regarding fortifying your properties and doing what is customary for you. If you have a greater actual bias, you might be better off performing the labor yourself. Dealing with a group of people to do the work for you may be your best option if your bias is less about the specifics of the project and more about the overall strategy.

This idea can be applied in two ways: determining the fundamental system you should pursue and considering how to structure your technique choice. To do anything specialized, you can choose a less factually biased contributing system from the outset. If you're excellent at more specialized work, you can choose a more specialized system, but you also have the option to rebuild that same system so that it allows you to transition from the specialized side to the master plan side.

In his books, Robert Kiyosaki clarifies the distinction between an entrepreneur and a representative in great detail. The difference between these two occupations is reappropriation. When you agree to outsource portions of your business, you begin to free yourself from having to perform all the dynamic work yourself. This is the entrepreneurial approach: learning how to become an entrepreneur as opposed to resigning oneself to being a laborer who does all the work.

You Do Not Need Landlording Experience to Manage a Landlord

Related to reevaluating occupations is the common misconception that you should always own your own property first, even if you intend to switch to utilizing a property manager. People advise you to do this so that you can better understand how to interact with the property manager.

They anticipate that if you have direct experience as a property owner, you will know what to look for in a property manager and will understand their day-to-day responsibilities, allowing you to determine whether or not they are handling their business correctly.

This would be valid if the correlation was consistent. Unfortunately, this is more of an apples-to-ham comparison. When you're a landlord, you need to accomplish the following: finding and supervising tenants, accepting service calls and planning repairs, knowing and upholding state and neighborhood laws applicable to the property, documenting and handling evictions, and having the capacity to investigate or issue settlements for various issues that may arise with the inhabitants or the property. When interacting with a property director, it is sufficient to know how to interact with the individual who is carrying out these tasks. You don't truly need to know how to complete any of these tasks; all you need to know is how to determine whether they are being completed satisfactorily. Indeed, one could argue that you would need to know how to perform those tasks in order to know what constitutes acceptable. However, as the landowner, if you continue to receive payment, see periodic property assessment records demonstrating that the property's condition is being maintained, and maintain communication with the property manager, you can reasonably assume that those tasks are being completed satisfactorily.

Again, it is not necessary to understand how these duties are being completed, only that they are being completed. For example, you do not need to understand the nuances of fixing a latrine; you only need to ensure that the latrine is repaired.

Knowing how to perform the itemized, unremarkable, or more mundane tasks of landlording will be of little assistance in coping with a property manager, as these tasks are extremely independent: managing specialized tasks as opposed to managing people.

Consider purchasing and maintaining a business. Imagine that instead of creating pizzas, you acquire a cupcake shop. You have no idea how to make cupcakes, and you have no interest in learning. You may not even know how to properly heat. You, as the business proprietor, are not required to know how to bake cupcakes, so long as you are able to retain employees who do. There is a good chance that these individuals know how to make cupcakes better than you ever could. To keep the business thriving, it is your responsibility to maintain a consistent focus on the big picture, perform business responsibilities, ensure that all of your employees are functioning correctly, and ensure that everything runs smoothly. It is not necessary to know how to bake cupcakes for that to occur.

Consider the opposite situation, where the best cupcake maker in town is urged to establish their own cupcake shop. The most common reason a system like this fails is that the person who is so skilled at making cupcakes also needs to run a business, which is unrelated to cupcake making. They are not even in the same domain of ability ranges. Due to the fact that the responsibilities of an entrepreneur are vastly different from those of a baker, the cupcake expert presently loses their business or becomes hopeless managing it.

It points in both directions: business minds typically do not do well in specialized positions, and specialized personalities can struggle with business endeavors. Neither set of abilities is superior or inferior to the other; they are simply distinct. Individuals typically lack an understanding of how skill ranges fluctuate and which jobs are required, causing them to unknowingly undertake tasks outside of their skill set.

There are, however, successful cupcake entrepreneurs who are exceptionally skilled at baking cupcakes and therefore prepare a substantial portion of the cupcakes for their shop. This resembles the situation I mentioned previously in which the owner must be available to generate revenue. This would be comparable to being a proprietor of your own property. You are the entrepreneur (financial supporter), but you are also skilled at performing the specialized work (landlording), so you do it on your own and do not require assistance from anyone else.

If you will likely operate a cupcake realm in the future, however, and your focus is on the business rather than baking cupcakes, you should focus on learning how to manage the people and players who make up your domain. You won't have the time or capacity to build the domain if you're too busy baking cupcakes.

If you appreciate being a landlord and you're not necessarily looking to expand your portfolio, you should learn how to be a landlord. You are not obligated to stick with one option or the other; you can ultimately switch to property managers if necessary. But if you never want to be a landlord and are more interested in building an empire, then learning how to handle maintenance requests and evict a tenant does not prepare you to construct and manage an empire.

Then, what abilities do you need to acquire? That depends on your long-term objective. You are free to take on landlording tasks in order to gain experience or to act as a proprietor for a time. However, mastering landlording tasks is not a prerequisite for managing property managers. In addition to not being a requirement, it is also a disconnected set of skills.

Expansion Will Forever Be Restricted

To construct a domain, it is not sufficient to possess advanced business skills; you must also possess the capacity to expand.

You can indeed reverse a limited number of properties simultaneously if you flip properties and do the majority of the work yourself. But if you have a team assisting you with the various aspects of the flip, you can work on multiple initiatives simultaneously. Similar restrictions apply if you are a landlord; you can only own a limited number of properties by yourself. If you require more properties than you can own on your own, you will need to enlist the assistance of others.

When you accomplish nearly everything on your own, you restrict the amount that should be possible at once.

I recall working as a designer in a corporate environment. If I were a one-person operation, I would only be able to complete a limited number of design jobs at once. But if I assumed a management position and employed engineers to assist with my projects, I would be able to take on a number of engineering projects limited only by the number of employees I have.

If you're doing everything you can to avoid becoming a realm-claiming hotshot and you enjoy doing the work yourself, there's nothing wrong with that. It has to do with understanding your limitations and whether or not they will prevent you from achieving something you're endeavoring. If you want to grow but are unwilling to stop trying to manage everything on your own, your development will be limited.

Real Estate Investment Secrets

Migration to the area, population growth, transportation enhancements, nearby institutions, unemployment rates, employment growth, and nearby businesses are a few of the most important factors to consider. If you invest in these areas, you will prosper in the longer term.

Be open to working with a variety of financial sponsors and arrangements. When you have companions, you can take advantage of opportunities that you wouldn't otherwise be able to.

With partners, you can zero in on the parts of the plan that match your abilities or objectives.

You may need to investigate effective land-based financial supporters. They have knowledge and experience in this field.

As a land financial supporter, you should evaluate all opportunities for generating income. You can invest in investment properties, flip deteriorating residences, and trade commercial properties.

Land financiers with experience investigate all options and do not limit themselves to a single revenue stream.

Diversification is an excellent method for increasing expected returns and spreading risk.

You should have an outstanding understanding of the market and the most common method of valuing properties. Examine the properties without contributing in earnest. Be objective and rational in order to make sensible decisions.

Options

It is a contract that allows a financial supporter to trade an instrument over a specified period of time.

You retain the right to exercise this option until the contract's expiration date. It is optional; therefore, you do not have to practice it if you do not need to.

Options belong among the larger collections of protections known as subsidiaries. It is termed a subsidiary because its cost is subject to or derived from the cost of something else.

Note that choices are not as ancient as they were because they do not address company responsibility.

At any time, you may terminate or exit a contract with options. The choice's price is a level of the essential resource or security.

It entails determining the probabilities of future value events. Varieties of choices:

• Call Feature. It is an agreement that grants the financial supporter the option to purchase a predetermined quantity of a specific security or item at a predetermined price over a predetermined time period. In this circumstance, you need the stock price to increase so that you can profit from your agreement by exercising your right to buy the stock and selling it fast for a profit.

- Put Options. It is an agreement that provides the financial backer the option to sell a predetermined number of units of a specific security or good at a predetermined price over a predetermined period of time. To generate a profit in this circumstance, the security's price must decline, or you must sell the put option if you believe the price will rise.

Options are also referred to as:

American options. Your option may be exercised at any time between the date of purchase and the expiration date. Due to the value of the option to practice early, American options typically command a higher premium than European options.

European options. They must be utilized near the end of their existence on their expiration date.

In both call-out and put options, you can exercise your right to sell or buy up until the agreement's expiration date. Charges will increase proportionally to the remaining duration of the agreement.

You can reinstate the agreement after it has expired. This could be on a weekly, monthly, or quarterly basis.

The benefits of alternatives are as follows: • They are cost-effective; • They have exceptional yield potential; and • They pose less risk.

The disadvantages are reduced liquidity, high commissions, and time decay. The value of your chosen premium decreases daily by specific rates

Simply trade options through a business. You would also be required to pay the fee (premium) to acquire the contract.

First, select the resource that will serve as your concealed resource. Then, you must decide whether you believe the stock price will increase or decrease.

Futures are monetary subsidiary contracts that bind parties to exchange a resource at a predetermined future date and price.

The purchaser must purchase or the seller must sell the resource at the predetermined price, regardless of the current market price at the termination date. The dealers secure in the asset's price.

A prospects contract enables an investor to speculate on the direction of a security, product, or financial instrument.

Futures are subordinate because their value is contingent on a secret resource.
• Commodity prospects. Ex: crude oil, combustible gas, grain, and wheat

• Stock index futures • Currency futures
• Precious metal futures. The precious metals gold and silver

- Prospects for US depository bonds and other products

What is the distinction between options and outcomes? In choices, the agreements allow the holder to trade the resources at any time prior to the expiration date. In a fates contract, the purchaser is obligated to retrieve the product at the contract's expiration.

As with options, the buyer of a prospects agreement may sell their situation at any time prior to expiration and be released from their obligation. The financial backer is not required to put up 100 percent of the agreement's value upon commencing the transaction. The agent would require a modest deposit, a fraction of the total agreement value.

If a vendor purchased a contract from a prospect and the cost of the item exceeded the initial agreement's value, they would make a profit.

Speculators may also sell if they anticipate that the resource's price will decline. Futures Advantages: • Simple Pricing • High Liquidity

Disadvantages of futures: • Absence of control over future events • Price fluctuations • Potential reduction in resource cost as expiration date approaches

To invest in destinies, an agent is required. Several prospective business sectors trade after normal market hours.

When a position is closed, exceptionally minimal commissions are charged for futures exchanges.

Not Always Is The Grass Greener

In some regions, prices for lFurthermore are significantly greater than in others. And, for land investors who wish to own income-producing properties but reside in extremely expensive regions, it can be extremely alluring to seek for greener pastures far from home. Gina was limited to this type of financial supporter. She needed the benefits that long-term land ownership could provide, including steady monthly income, appreciation, and tax benefits as devaluation, the increase in value from occupants paying off the mortgage with each monthly lease payment, and perhaps the appreciation that land regularly displays.

She believed she had discovered a solution to her problem by purchasing properties in various industries that were already rented and had a manager in place. Generally referred to as turn-key properties, these arrangements required only a buyer, as all other details were likely already taken care of. As they were already rented, this aided in procuring contracts, and within a few months she was the proud owner of a property more than 500 miles away. She had invested 20% and her calculations predicted a return of 8%, which was significantly higher than the returns from her other investments. The best aspect was that she had enough money left over to purchase three similar properties. If she had attempted to buy something locally, she could have purchased no more than one property.

Not always is the grass greener. The tenant stopped paying rent, and Gina began making void house payments while she figured out how the eviction interaction worked. It turned out that the rent had been affected by the absence of a few critical statements, and it took an additional couple of months to legally evict the non-paying tenant. In addition, they left the property in shambles. The property manager hired a contractor who charged tens of thousands of dollars to re-carpet and repaint the home, in addition to a few other renovations.

Gina took out her minicomputer once more and realized that it would take three years of income to make up for everything she had lost due to the departure of one tenant. She witnessed firsthand how costly a vacant single-family home can be for the owner, as well as how overly optimistic her 8% return estimate was for this investment. She decided to simply sell it in order to swiftly recover from her misfortunes. She was astounded to discover that the price she had paid for the property far exceeded what it would fetch on the open market. She failed to consider the price tag in relation to the property's actual market value because she was preoccupied with how inexpensive the total cost was in comparison to the land prices in her previous neighborhood. Gina was deceived into believing that the property she was purchasing was a good deal due to the fact that it cost one-fourth as much as a comparable home in her previous neighborhood. In all other respects, she was learning through adversity the price difference between a neighborhood investment and another investment. It is the true market value of the property, as determined by comparable sales of comparable properties in the vicinity and compared to the purchase price.

It also occurred to her why the seller of the property was selling to someone 500 miles away rather than someone in the community. They certainly knew the adage PT Barnum coined, "Every day a sucker is born." Due to the relatively high rental rates relative to property costs (and by adding a fourth room), the previous owner had the option of selling the property for a higher price to a buyer from a significant distance (new to the neighborhood) as a turnkey rental than to a local retail buyer seeking to make it their primary residence.

Gina was also perplexed as to how the appraiser hired by the moneylender when she purchased the property could have valued it at the entire purchase price when, nine months later, she was unable to sell it for anything close to what she had paid for it. She observed another excellent example. Appraisers frequently use the purchase price as a significant factor in determining the assessed value of a property. Consequently, she discovered that it is the responsibility of the purchaser to focus on comparable transactions and determine for themselves what a property would sell for if it were ever put up for sale. An inspection does not always precisely predict the price at which a property will sell when listed on the open market.

Not wanting to forfeit any of her 20% down payment, she decided to lease the property. Gina was ecstatic to learn that she had control over the decision regarding who would rent the property this time when the property manager presented her with two options of prospective tenants one month later. Also 10 purchase a property for in your former space does not determine the health of months that have passed without incident. And subsequently, the resident stopped paying, and the nightmare began again from the beginning. Fortunately, she had retained a few things from the initial ejection, so this subsequent one was not as severe. However, there were once more maintenance bills, and the expenses for this purported investment were consuming her personal funds.

After a month with no occupant, she decided to fly to the property and determine what was going on. She discovered that the property manager was barely marketing the unit to potential tenants. Gina was also shocked by the ineffectiveness of the work performed by the jack-of-all-trades. She personally witnessed the dangers of recruiting individuals without a means of holding them accountable.

Then, she dug deeper into the financial connections of the gatherings and discovered that the property manager was receiving a kickback for everything he did. Possibly even worse, she reviewed her agreement with the property manager and determined that since the manager received 100% of the first month's rent, or $1,000, but only $100, or 10% of each recurring payment thereafter, the manager received more cash flow as the occupants changed. Even if the property remained vacant for a couple of months, if the property manager made multiple times more each time a new tenant moved in, they would have significantly more cash flow than with a long-term paying tenant.

Gina had made a few mistakes, but she realized she desperately needed assistance. She limited the options to two alternatives. Either she would relinquish it and allow it to fall into disrepair, or she would contribute what little she had to pass on instructions to turn her boat around. She applied for and was accepted into the Freedom Mentor Apprentice Program (bold attachment of the creator's land financial backer coaching administration), and rather than throwing her hands up in the air and giving up, she decided to learn how to manage this arrangement and turn her past failure into a foundation for her future success.

Her instructor instructed her to take action. Initially, rather than re-leasing to an ordinary occupant, she was instructed to find a Tenant Buyer on a Rent-to-Own program who would not just be endeavoring to one day be the proprietor, yet would likewise set up a substantial nonrefundable option installment. She discovered that although the rental market was saturated, the demand for Rent-to-Own houses was tremendous, and she had the ability to quickly secure a Tenant Buyer with a $5,000 option payment who also had stable employment and excellent rental history. This additional $5,000 was instrumental in assisting her with the unmet house installments and repairs she needed to make after the previous occupants moved out. In addition, she chose a value that would prevent her from losing money.

Next, she hired another property manager to watch over the property, but had the option to negotiate a much lower monthly salary and eliminated the ability to receive payoffs from employees for hire. Then, as soon as the Tenant Buyers moved in, she connected them with a mortgage broker so they could immediately begin working to improve their financial situation so they could obtain a loan prior to the end of the option period.

A year later, she had the option to sell the property to the Tenant Buyers and walk away without losing her 20% down payment and without incurring any additional losses. No, she did not earn any money, but she eventually recouped her initial investment and gained something far more valuable from the experience. Gina now understood how to make shrewd investing decisions moving forward and continued to dominate as a real estate investor.

Effective and Beneficial Learning Lessons

(1) Usually, the vegetation is not greener elsewhere. Even with a property manager in place, owning large tracts of rental land can be extremely difficult and typically unprofitable in the long haul.

(2) The cost of a property proportional to the cost of land in your area is not an indicator of a community's health advantage. Even though the expense is low for you, this does not make it a wise decision. All purchase costs, no matter how large or small, must be compared to the property's market value in order to determine whether the property was purchased prudently.

(3) The finest hypotheses are NOT those that are presented with a royal flourish. Assuming it has been completely "done-

for-you," the arrangement is probably not as good as you might expect. According to Andrew Carnegie, "the first gets the pearl and the second gets the empty shell." The majority of turn-key real estate deals involve merchants snatching the jewels and selling you the empty shells.

Investing Pays

Now I will list a few individuals whose investments grew substantially over time. Everyone devised their own strategy. Everyone had a unique outlook on the market. They all invested and remained invested despite enduring numerous market ups and downs.

There are numerous hypotheses upon which investors make decisions. Benjamin Graham, a financial market expert whose book 'The Intelligent Investor' is read by the majority of investors with an interest in reading and in financial markets, popularized the concept of 'Value Investing', which is employed by certain investors.

Reading books, listening to financial experts, and listening to analysts is beneficial, but each individual has a unique perspective. They each express their opinions to the best of their ability, which is dependent on a variety of factors, including their fundamental nature, their way of thinking, and their professional and investing journeys.

A successful investor takes into account the other party's capabilities and capacities, analyzes his own capabilities and capacities, and then reaches a conclusion.

There are numerous interpretations of value investing, but the fundamental principle is that an investor purchases securities at a discount to their intrinsic value, maintaining a margin of safety. Whenever there is a market collapse, even shares of blue-chip companies are available at a price below their intrinsic value. A value investor takes advantage of this opportunity to purchase these securities.

When asked how he became so wealthy, Rothschild attributed his success to two factors. He stated, "He always bought when there was blood on the streets, panic, and chaos, and when despair grips the market, he sells too early, not waiting for the enthusiasm to peak."

This is yet another method for value investors. Rothschild was a German banker and the legendary House of Rothschild's progenitor.

Let's examine the precise definition of "Intrinsic Value and Margin of Safety."

Many stock market analysts believe that the market price of any particular share does not reflect the company's actual value. The analysts then determine whether the share price of a particular company is undervalued or overvalued based on its intrinsic value.

Intrinsic Value is the actual value of a security, the value of the underlying business that can be determined by analyzing all aspects of the business, including its actual net worth and other variables such as brand name, trademarks, and copyrights that frequently do not reflect in a company's financial statements. They are frequently difficult to calculate and are not always reflected accurately in the market price of a company.

Different investors use different methods to determine the intrinsic value of a company, and even when using the same data, they arrive at different figures. The reason they arrive at different numbers is because they use distinct formulas to calculate the value.

There are five widely used formulas for calculating the intrinsic value of a security. In value investing, calculating intrinsic value is the most important factor. Value investors anticipate purchasing shares when they are priced substantially below their intrinsic value.

Margin of Safety in value investing is the disparity between the purchase price and intrinsic value of a stock. When the market price of a stock is 20 to 40 percent below its intrinsic value, value investors seek to purchase the stock. The margin of safety provides a cushion in the event that an error was made in calculating the intrinsic value.

Many investors with a high risk tolerance favor the Growth Theory over the concept of value investing in order to generate greater market returns.

The growth theory is an investment strategy that considers the earnings development prospects of a stock in addition to its current market price.

The investors who choose this strategy have a positive outlook on life and on their decision. They believe in investing in businesses by visualizing their growth prospects in the future. They believe that the current price of a company's stock is the most reasonable price for that stock, and they wish to profit from the company's future development.

This debate has raged for many years over whether "investing for growth" or "investing for value" is more profitable, as the two theories are diametrically opposed.

Whereas value investors buy stocks at relatively low prices, as indicated by low price-to-earnings, price-to-book, and price-to-sales ratios, and high dividend yields, growth investors seek out stocks with high price-to-earnings, price-to-book, and price-to-sales ratios, and low dividend yields.

In the same way that he sells if he believes a stock is excessive and buys if he believes it is underpriced, a value investor will only purchase a stock if he believes it is mispriced. They are more patient than growth investors because they only invest when the market has crashed and is despondent. They seek for companies that are fundamentally sound but are performing poorly due to the cyclical nature of their industry, but are still performing reasonably well despite being at the bottom of the cycle.

In the past, value investors made a fortune. This may not function as well as it did in the past due to the rapid technological advancement of the world and the rapid evolution of all technologies. This has brought about significant changes to traditional business practices and investor consideration.

Chapter Five: Using the Money of Others

There is always the option of using cash as currency, but rather than using your own money, you can use someone else's. This is sometimes referred to as "utilizing" or "utilizing" OPM: others' money.

OPM may originate from a variety of sources, including but not limited to institutions.

credit associations

private financiers

credit cards

investment associates

seller-financing

relatives & acquaintances

In addition to the obvious case of not having enough of your own money to contribute, so you must use another person's money, there is also the case of having enough of your own money to contribute but choosing to use another person's money anyway. Why would you contemplate doing that if you could just use your own money? Two factors:

1. Eventually, you will run out of your own money, forcing you to cease investing.

2. Profits from influencing the finances of others have an infinitely greater yield potential.

Eventually running out of money is a reality. You have a limited pool of assets, and once that pool is depleted, it's over. Utilizing other people's money, either exclusively or in addition to your own, is the best method to grow your wealth beyond what you already have.

However, a higher yield potential? This may require further explanation. How is it possible that I could achieve greater returns by investing with someone else's money, especially given the current market?

supposing I'm paying a return on the acquired funds?

Using Mathematics

You acquire a $100,000 investment property with actual cash. You collect $1000 per month in rent and $700 per month after expenses. Calculating the money oncash return on that yields an 8.4% return on investment.

As opposed to paying cash, you now finance the purchase of a $100,000 investment property. The property's rent and expenses are the same as before, but you must now deduct $430 per month for the contract fee. Currently, your net monthly income is only $270 per month. But when you compare that $270/month to the difference between a $20,000 down payment and that $270/month, you would have saved $20,000.

$100,000 (20% upfront payment as opposed to completing the complete purchase price in cash), your cash-on-cash return increases to 16.2%.

Utilizing this $100,000 investment property provides you with a

16.2% return on your investment while purchasing it outright yields only a

8.4% return on your money. You've recently increased profits. Moreover, these are only the income returns.

Since you just spent $20,000 on a $100,000 property using a mortgage, and assuming you have $100,000 to invest (which is why you considered possibly paying cash), you could purchase five properties instead of having the option to purchase one for $100,000.

Using the same numbers as above, if you have five properties earning $270 per month, you are currently receiving $1,350 per month. Consequently, for the same

$100,000 investment ($100,000 cash invested in one property or $100,000 divided among five properties with a 20% down payment on each), you will generate a higher monthly income.

But there's more to come.

In addition to income, investment property can generate returns from appreciation, tax savings, value accumulation through contract paydown, and indirect returns when the property serves as a hedge against inflation.

Say, in terms of precise appreciation, your $100,000 home appreciates to $150,000. You have acquired a value of $50,000, which is essentially free money. If you purchased a single property, you would have recently gained $50,000. Consider the possibility that you purchased five of these properties and that they all increased in value by

$50,000? You would have acquired $250,000 in free money ($50,000 profit multiplied by five properties) rather than $50,000.

There is a significant difference between $250,000 and $50,000, and the bank is not keeping that currency; it is yours. Increased monthly income and fivefold appreciation. Add five times the tax benefits and five times the equity built through mortgage paydown, and all of these properties are inflation-hedging. Then you have incorporated risk mitigation against vacancy as well, because if one property becomes vacant, the income from the other four properties will keep you afloat during the vacancy period.

Despite the fact that the cited figures are not inclusive of all of the costs associated with purchasing a home, they demonstrate the financial power of utilizing. You are observing multiple times the monetary impact of your conjecture due to the fact that you are able to use your money.

Innovative Finance Options

There are alternatives to conventional home loans for utilizing funds. In reality, one of the most significant factors that distinguishes successful realm developers from other financial supporters is their ability to devise creative methods of utilizing capital. Many people do not begin with a substantial amount of money to invest, and they may not satisfy all requirements for a mortgage or credit. What are these people doing? Indeed, this is where the 'innovative' component enters into play. Assuming you can devise methods to intelligently back deals, you will likely be on the road to success.

I can give you an example of something I did in the early years of my real estate investment career. After the collapse in Nicaragua, I was in need of funds. But a few opportunities arose that I was eager to take advantage of. At that time, I had approximately $10,000 to contribute. In 2011, when the recession was still in full swing, I could purchase an exceptional investment property with $10,000 and a mortgage without much difficulty. I realized I could do this for one property, but once the $10,000 was gone, how could I purchase additional properties?

Hello, innovative financing!

I acquired a venture partner for multiple properties at this period.

The investment partner had various arrangements of $10,000 available. What then could I

what can you offer him in compensation for his money? We agreed to purchase the deals with his cash and my credit. He covered the initial payments, while I took out the mortgages in my name and completed everything else. Therefore, he contributed the funds, and I created the risk. We agreed that this indicated a 50/50 division in commitment. So, when we purchased the properties, we divided everything down the middle 50/50, regardless of whether it was a benefit or a disadvantage. Consistently, when we collected revenue, he received half and I received the other half. Assuming that significant costs arose, we divided them in half. If we decided to sell, we would divide the profit or loss equally. As far as he was concerned, this arrangement was ideal because he was able to save money without incurring any penalties or losing contract capacity (you can obtain a limited number of home loans in your name). In addition, I ended up with virtually unlimited returns because I invested no capital in the properties.

That is just one of the numerous options for creative financing solutions. Other financing options may incorporate non-conventional mortgage credits. It is possible to transfer value from one property to another. There are countless opportunities for funding speculations. The key is to ensure you are aware of the specifics of each option and to choose one that seems appropriate for your situation.

Developing creative financial arrangements is ostensibly the essence of constructing a domain. You can acquire some useful knowledge from individuals who have already completed the task independently, but they can only take you so far. Ultimately, you must determine a great deal of it on your own. Sorting out creative financing arrangements is essentially a rite of passage for successful financial backers; almost no domain proprietors make progress without creative financing.

The Danger

There are one million arguments regarding the dangers of substance abuse. When done irresponsibly, using other people's money is extremely hazardous.

For instance, you might use a flexible rate advance to acquire an investment property. The property is initially profitable and productive. However, the rate change appears out of nowhere, and the premium rate suddenly increases.

skyrockets. Currently, you are in a negative income situation, which is just one of many accumulating issues.

Another model assumes that a hard currency advance is utilized for a flip. You obtain the cash, which typically comes with an exorbitant loan fee because it's a short-term advance, and the flip project suddenly takes a turn for the worse — for example, the recovery cost becomes prohibitive so you can't complete the venture, and now you can't sell the property for what was agreed upon — and the advance result is expected.

However, if you know what you're doing and you're smart about how you structure your utilizing, you can significantly reduce utilizing risks.

Obtaining a fixed-rate credit rather than a variable-rate loan is the obvious choice for this investment property. If you combine a fixed-rate loan with the property's location in a strong growth area with the ability to attract high-quality residents, your utilizing risks diminish significantly.

To minimize risk when flipping a property with hard cash, despite the fact that the basic structure does not alter, it is essential to understand precisely what you are doing as a flipper. The concept of flipping is straightforward: purchase a distressed property, restore it, and sell it for a profit.

However, converting can be fraught with numerous obstacles that new investors are unaware of. These unexpected difficulties can place the financial backer in grave peril of being unable to repay the advance. Another method for mitigating risk in this circumstance is to establish a backup plan for credit restitution in the event that the flip does not go as planned.

"»»

There's no denying that using other people's money in real estate investing is not only incredibly lucrative, but also required in a number of situations to continue developing your portfolio. In the end, however, monetary success is a variable metric, just like any type of development. A person's perception of advancement and another person's perception of accomplishment may be absurdly dissimilar. There are some individuals who are content with maintaining modest portfolios. There are also individuals who may feel so uncomfortable with using — using other people's money — that no amount of financial success justifies the weight they may place on it. In neither of these instances is it necessary to be reckless with money.

innovativeness. However, if you do decide to take advantage of the opportunity to use other people's money in your contributions, you genuinely open the door to limitless growth.

Investment Funds

You are not investing on your own in an asset. There is a pool of investors who contribute money to an aggregate investment.

It is a safer option than purchasing stocks because you are not bearing the risk on your own.

By utilizing an asset, you have access to a greater number of investment opportunities, more administration expertise to assist you, and reduced investment costs than if you were investing on your own.

You do not make individual decisions regarding how the asset's resources should be allocated. You choose an asset based on its objectives, risk, and expenses.

A manager of the asset determines which protections it should hold, in what quantities, and when the protections should be traded. Consequently, you benefit from superior administrative expertise.

You are acquiring shares of this asset. The majority of assets have a specific theme:
- Geographical
- Industrialization
- Varieties of investments
- Size of the firm

There are also numerous types of funds:
- Mutual funds
- Index funds
- Exchange-exchanged funds
- Money market funds
- Hedge funds

The advantages of venture reserves include:
They carry various items.
• Easy to store away
• A professional cashier is required for the shipment.
• Low acquisition cost

The disadvantages are:
• The costs
• Performance or rate of return are not assured.
• You cannot change your investment because the asset manager has control.

You should contribute for a minimum of five years. If you anticipate needing immediate access to your funds, then this may not be the best investment for you.

Utilizing an asset grocery store or stages is the most cost-effective method for depositing funds into reserves. They are available online.

Investing in reserves involves two stages. Initially, you must determine which platform you will use; then, you must decide which project to incorporate.

You will incur fees for both using the platform and purchasing the funds.

Mutual Funds

A shared asset is an asset type. They are investment vehicles that allow you to merge your funds with those of other investors to purchase a variety of stocks, securities, and other investments. Notably, a financial supporter of a common asset does not possess the protections to which the asset contributes; they only own portions of the asset itself.

You may trade your asset shares once per day at the close of the market for all shared assets. The price fluctuates based on the value of the asset's components at the end of each business day.

You can earn money in three possible ways:
- Income derived from share dividends
- Coupon on bonds
- A rise in the price of protections. If the asset share price is

If the fund grows, you can sell your shares for a profit. There are four types of common funds:
- Those who invest capital in shares (value reserves). They invest in corporate proposals by purchasing shares of a variety of publicly traded companies. They have a greater

development potential, but experience cost fluctuations.

- Bonds (fixed-remuneration reserves). The most popular type of fixed pay common assets. Financial supporters are repaid a reasonable amount for their investment in the enterprise. The securities reserve invests in government and corporate debt. They are viewed as a more secure investment than stocks but have less growth potential than value funds. These reserves are frequently well-managed and seek to purchase somewhat undervalued securities to sell for a profit.
- Money market (temporary liability). It consists of secure short-term obligations, typically government Treasury bills. This is a secure location to store your currency. You will not

receive substantial returns, but you will not need to worry about losing your initial investment. The average return is somewhat greater than the amount you would obtain from a standard checking or investment account.

• Stocks and bonds. The objective is to reduce risk by investing in both. diversifying.

• Income reserve. Consistently, they generate current income. These assets are primarily invested in government and high-quality corporate debt, retaining these securities until development generates interest payments. Consequently, they are longer range. However, their primary objective is to generate a steady income for their financial supporters. Common financial supporters are moderate, retired individuals. Charge-aware financial supporters may want to steer clear of these funds because they generate standard pay.

Each common asset is designed to mitigate risk while capturing business sector gains.

The benefits of mutual funds:

- You gain the benefit of having an expert supervisor continuously evaluate your portfolio.
- The cost of the exchange is divided among all investors in the asset, reducing the cost per investor.
- Mutual assets invest in a wide spectrum of areas, immediately differentiating the portfolio.

The obstacles are:

- Costly fees
- Fiscal inefficacy

- inadequate exchange execution
- Possibility of board abuse

Mutual assets may be acquired directly from a shared asset organization, a bank, or a financial institution. Before making a donation, you should create an account.

There are a variety of costs that may be associated with common funds. Some assets are accompanied by exchange fees or commissions for trading. Annual asset operating expenses are a yearly proportion of the managed assets.

Some assets incur a recovery cost if you sell shares you've only held for a brief duration.

As with any endeavor, there are also risks involved. There is always a possibility that the value of your common asset will decline. Mutual assets are typically more appropriate for long-term investors.

If you anticipate needing your funds shortly, a mutual fund may not be the best choice. This is because the return in that amount of time (after deducting the cost of fees) may not be sufficient to make the investment worthwhile.

Index Funds

A record store is a business that monitors a market file (for example, the S&P 500, the top 500 stocks in the United States).

Typically, they consist of equities or bonds. There is a record and a list reserve for virtually every financial market in existence.

The superintendent of assets constructs a portfolio whose assets reflect the protections of a particular index.
It attempts to replicate the development and execution of a financial market program. It means to match rather than surpass its
performance.
It is similar to a shared or trade-exchanged asset.
(ETF). To spend:
Choose the file. There are numerous files that can be followed using file reserves. You can also view area records associated with specific businesses, country files that target equities in single countries, and style files that highlight rapidly growing companies.
• Select a fund
• Buy stocks

The advantages are:
- Broad market openness. There are file archives accessible for a variety of endeavors. Stock record assets and security list funds are available for purchase.
- Low operating expenses. They have a reduced proportion of board costs. The administrator of record subsidizes property exchanges less frequently, resulting in lower exchange fees and commissions.
- Low portfolio liquidity

You can contribute with reduced risk. Most accounts contain dozens or even hundreds of stocks and other investments, and the increase in diversification makes you more resistant to significant losses.

- Since they employ a hands-off approach to investment, they incur lower costs and fees than actively managed reserves. The file store manager must acquire the securities or other interests in a file. He is not required to identify specific performing securities.
- You will incur fewer expenses. In comparison to numerous other investments, they have a high rate of return.

These are the obstacles to a record store speculation:

- You will never outperform the market. They are designed to mirror the performance of the market.
- You have no misfortune protection. When the market plummets, your list asset will plummet as well, as list assets

follow their respective business sectors through a variety of difficulties.
• You will not own your favorite stocks eternally.
• No authority over holdings
Generally, the speculation will be conducted over an extended period of time to stimulate positive performance. Investors make an initial minimum investment ($3,000 - $10,000) and pay annual expenses to maintain the asset (a small proportion of the capital invested). You can purchase a list reserve directly from a common asset organization or a financial institution. To purchase shares in your preferred list store, you can establish an account directly with the common asset organization offering the fund.
Exchange-Traded Funds (ETFs)

It is a collection of businesses that are sold on a market. Similar to individual equities, ETF shares are traded throughout the day at prices that fluctuate based on supply and demand. The asset supplier claims the resources, designs an asset to follow their presentation, and then solicits investors for stakes in that asset.

Shareholders own a portion of an ETF, but they do not own the underlying assets.

The primary distinction between ETFs and common assets is that ETF shares trade throughout the trading day, whereas shares of mutual funds only trade once a day after the market closes. ETFs have become ubiquitous investments. Due to their many benefits, including low cost proportions, liquidity, venture scope, and a low speculation threshold, they are ideal for beginning investors.

Types of exchange-traded funds:

• Bond. It may include government, corporate, and civil securities. Security ETFs detest individual internet-based securities because they lack a maturity date, so their most common use is to produce recurring cash payments to the financial backer. These payments are derived from the interest generated by the individual securities within the fund.

• Businesses. Observe a particular industry

• Products. Invest in commodities such as crude petroleum or gold

The monetary system. Put resources into unfamiliar currencies

A trade-exchanged asset has a price that facilitates its purchase and sale.

You can have an actively managed ETF where portfolio managers are more involved with trading portions of companies; however, an actively managed asset will have higher expenses than an inactively managed asset.

Benefits of ETFs:

- They provide investors with the ability to acquire as stock prices rise and decline
- Investors can benefit from dividend-paying companies.
- Investors in ETFs are eligible for a portion of the earnings
- Flexible. During the day, when business sectors are accessible, ETFs are traded.

- They provide diversification for a portfolio
- Lower price. They are passively due, with significantly reduced cost ratios compared to funds that are actively managed.
- Tax benefits. Due to underlying differences, shared assets incur higher capital charges than ETFs. They have smaller capital additions and are payable upon the ETF's issuance.

Disadvantages of ETFs:
- Subject to display variation
- Subject to administrative expenses and other costs
- The cost could be greater. Assuming that you compare ETFs and investing in a specific stock,

inventory expenses are higher

ETFs are traded through online specialists and traditional representative dealers. You must establish a corporate account.

Money Market Funds

It is a type of common asset that invests in extremely liquid, short-term instruments. They are expected to provide investors with a high degree of dissolvability and an exceedingly low degree of risk.

A venture store company supports the conjecture that is a currency market reserve.

A currency market reserve generates income but minimal capital appreciation, implying that the underlying investment appreciates minimally.

Money market accounts are a wise investment if you can maintain a high minimum balance, limit your withdrawals, and understand that you are not protected against inflation. They are divided into the following categories:

- Prime liquid assets. Invests non-depository assets in floating-rate obligations and business paper.

The government's currency on hand. Contributes nearly 99.5% of its total assets to actual money and government securities.

- Government reserve. Invest in conventional US depository obligation securities
- Non-taxable cash store. Offer income exempt from U.S. taxation

The benefits of currency market funds are:

- Excellent location to stop currency for the present. Safer due to the fact that these types of assets invest in generally safe vehicles. Consistently generates a low single-digit return for investors.
- They invest in extremely fluid security measures. This indicates that financial backers can transfer them easily.

The obstacles are:

- Purchasing power is resilient. They can generate returns under expansion, resulting in diminished purchasing power.
- Fees can consume a substantial portion of the benefit. Usually, a minimum balance is required to avoid a monthly service fee.

- They are not protected by the government. In the event that the investment reserve company becomes bankrupt, you may lose all of your money.
- Low-priced premium
- Inflation danger

Generally, you should pay tax on the premium you receive or the profits generated by the assets as you acquire them. Unless they are held in a tax-exempt retirement account.

In contrast to certificates of deposit, currency market accounts can be closed at any time without penalty.

You can purchase currency market assets from investment firms, financial institutions, and banks.

Hedge Funds

A multifaceted investment is an aggregated speculative reserve that trades relatively fluid resources and can employ more complex trading to improve performance.

A mutual fund's speculation administrator is typically paid an administration fee and a presentation fee.

Investors in speculative stock investments must be qualified (wealthy) monetary supporters.

are believed to be aware of the speculation risks and to acknowledge them because of the potential returns. The primary goals of speculative stock investments are to maximize returns and reduce risk. They intend to attempt to generate income regardless of the market's direction.

They are frequently readily available to authorized financial supporters. To be considered a certified financial supporter, you must meet one of the following requirements:
- Have an individual pay at least $200,000 for you alone
- You must have personal assets worth more than $1 million
- Must be a superior (chief, chief) involved in diversified investments or have a representative benefit plan or trust fund worth $5 million

The majority of speculative stock investments use a 2 and 20 administrator compensation plan, which provides the mutual fund manager 2% of the assets and a motivational expense of 20%.

Types:

- Macro. Invest in equities, bonds, destinies, alternatives, and occasionally currencies.
- Justice. Attempts to hedge against market value declines by investing in equities or stock files and then selling them.
- Relative value exchange for diverse investments. Purchase protections that are anticipated to increase in value, while selling those that are likely to depreciate.
- Troubled mutual funds. They are frequently associated with credit payments or reorganization.

Hedging reserves invest in real estate, real estate, monetary forms, subordinates, and others. Therefore, they can invest in anything.

The benefits of a support fund are:

- Adaptability. Individuals cannot freely trade mutual funds; as a result, they are more adaptable because there is no centralized body administering their performance.
- Aggressive conjecture technique. This is necessary to achieve a higher return.
- Enhances the likelihood of enhancement. The asset can increase diversification and reduce risk further.
- Guidance from knowledgeable professionals and candor. The flexible investing administrators are also versed in financial administration issues.

These are the disadvantages of speculative stock investments:

- Hedging store costs. Their pricing structure is known as 2 and 20. Financial backers pay a two percent administration fee for the asset's duties.

In addition, they pay the asset manager a 20% exhibition fee on any profits earned throughout the year.

• Risks and expected returns. They are considered to be taking so many risks.

• They are typically less volatile than securities or bonds

• You may only be able to withdraw your funds after having contributed for a certain period of time or at certain times of the year.

The minimum initial investment amounts for mutual funds range from $100,000 to over $2 million.

Individual investors have a very difficult time gaining access to high-quality mutual funds, but it is possible to invest in one through a circuitous route. You could invest in the stock of a financial institution that operates fence funds.

You Need Not Take A Vacation

Lifestyle Assets are vacation real estate investments. However, not every short-term rental qualifies as a Lifestyle Asset. There are three important factors that qualify a home as a Lifestyle Asset, which I will discuss in detail in the following section.

It is an undeniable fact that land has produced more than 90 percent of the world's tycoons. Nonetheless, land contribution is a vast ocean with a plethora of options. The masters of simple money use land investing to target those who seek to make a quick buck every day.

Recently, another type of real estate has gained popularity among investors: vacation rentals. You have probably heard of them or even stayed in one. They are typically vacation residences that are rented for less than 30 days at a time, and they can generate substantially higher returns than conventional long-term rental properties.

Airbnb, Vrbo, and countless other vacation rental marketplaces are acquiring control of the accommodation industry. With this rise in prominence comes a rise in deception and trickery surrounding this type of land speculation. I have owned a number of summer residences over the years, which Teresa and I have enjoyed with our families and friends. However, until recently I never contemplated renting any of them out as a present-day rental.

My family and I visited Bryce and Zion National Parks in Utah one summer. We discovered a property on vrbo.com and rented it for a week. When we arrived at the residence, it was incomprehensible. It was enormous and had breathtaking views of the surrounding regions. Large amusement rooms, a beautiful fire pit, and a hot tub. Everything in the residence was of the highest quality. I was unable to believe that this $1.5–2 million home was a rental because I was aware of property valuations. I estimated that it was likely the owner's primary residence and that they were merely renting it out at the time because they were absent.

On this trip, we were extremely unhappy with the hot tub, and the owner ended up coming to repair it. I complimented him on his excellent home, and he began telling me about the other one he was building right down the street that we should check out.

Then, he began to explain that this was solely an investment property and that he and his wife resided in a community approximately ten minutes away. He was so enthusiastic to inform me that he was on track to have these properties paid off in a reasonable amount of time using his income from short-term rentals.

I was somewhat surprised because, as far as I could tell, these types of residences did not make for exceptional investment properties. That was my initial introduction to the potential outcomes of the short-term vacation rental market as a real estate investment. Since then, my perspectives and abilities regarding this type of real estate investment have developed substantially.

I must be crystal clear that Lifestyle Assets is a time-consuming system for accumulating wealth. However, they can substantially increase your lifestyle freedom right now. In real estate, you typically build wealth and independence from the rat race through long-term arrangements, as opposed to short-term arrangements.

Regarding everyone, I created the term Lifestyle Assets. There are three significant factors that distinguish a Lifestyle Asset from a vacation rental property.

Lifestyle assets must be ready-to-use. I'm eager to enhance my lifestyle and independence from the office race. I would prefer not to be a property manager. Lifestyle Assets must qualify to be managed by a vacation administration organization. These organizations are extremely knowledgeable about the real estate market and your property. They will market your property. They will provide 24/7 five-star support for your site's visitors. They inspect and sanitize your property before and after guests arrive and depart. They collect the cash and goods from your guests. In general, they involve ensuring that your property complies with neighborhood and public facilitating laws and regulations.

Currently, many would-be investors are entering the market for short-term vacation rentals. They are quickly realizing the depressing truth that many regions do not permit investment properties. This should never occur if you have a cycle to follow when locating desirable areas that permit short-term rentals.

Lifestyle assets should pay for themselves. One property out of every odd number can eventually pay for itself. Lifestyle Assets do precisely this. I enjoy having someone else pay my mortgage. When we advise you on the best properties to purchase, you will bring so much joy to the lives of your guests.

They will appreciate the extraordinary property you allowed them to visit and enjoy with their families. They are delighted to cover your travel expenses, which reduce your mortgage and put money in your purse. It creates a shared benefit for all parties involved, and you can continue to build your portfolio with additional Lifestyle Assets that pay for themselves.

Lifestyle assets can be used for personal purposes. What is the point of owning properties that you do not use? We are here to construct a lifestyle. We are here to create lifestyle opportunities and freedom from the rat race. We ONLY purchase properties that we are interested in visiting ourselves. When assisting clients with the acquisition of Lifestyle Assets, one of the initial questions I pose to them is: Where do they enjoy deploying energy? I have claimed theoretical resources such as equities, tangible resources such as long-term rentals, fix-and-flip investments, and rudimentary land bargains. Despite generating income with these resources, I was unable to utilize them for my own benefit. I have never had more fun than when I am purchasing properties that I am eager to use and that enhance my lifestyle, and when I am assisting my clients in purchasing residences that they are eager to use and that enhance their lifestyle.

This essentially clarifies the three distinguishing characteristics between a Lifestyle Asset and a temporary vacation rental.

Stock Picking

Stay Away from Penny Stocks

Penny equities are popular among investors because they are inexpensive and can generate significant momentum. These two characteristics make them a favorite among small-budget traders. However, it is precisely because of these characteristics that investors should avoid penny securities. It is extremely difficult to predict the stock's movement, and the majority of penny stock companies are dubious.

As a beginner, you should remain focused on trading reliable stocks with a track record of success. Avoid penny securities, regardless of who may encourage you to invest in them.

Traits to Search For Liquidity

Poor liquidity is by far the most challenging aspect of the market from the perspective of a trader. Liquidity in the stock market refers to the daily volume or number of shares traded. If a stock has poor liquidity, it would be difficult to sell the stock or square off your position in that stock.

Poorly liquid stocks are also susceptible to manipulation. Even a small number of large traders can generate phony momentum in these securities, and you may fall victim to this trap.

An additional significant issue with limited liquidity stocks is wider spreads. The disparity between the bid price and the ask price is so great that the majority of traders cannot terminate their positions profitably.

In the outset, you must select only highly liquid stocks.

Consider Volatility

The stock market's volatility is not a negative thing. Good equities should have a certain level of volatility so that you can make money trading them in a single session. If the market as a whole or a particular stock has become extremely volatile due to news, results, litigation, or any other positive or negative information, you should avoid trading in such a stock. Certain strategies can assist you in earning money through options trading, but when a stock's volatility is high, trading can be extremely hazardous.

Most of the action in a stock with a high degree of volatility occurs within a few minutes, and by the time the majority of day traders enter the stock, it has already begun to move in the opposite direction. Therefore, it is preferable to avoid such chaos and allow the market to calm a bit before placing a trade. As a novice, you must maintain a focus on normal market transactions.

Excellent Correlation Stocks

Despite the fact that the stock market is driven by uncertainty, every trader favors reliable equities. It is always simpler for a day trader to map stocks that do not experience erratic price movement. These stocks are referred to as Correlative Stocks due to their extremely high correlation with the movement of specific sectors, indices, and market segments.

As a novice trader, you should also prioritize equities that are not very volatile. They may not make sudden or erratic movements, but that will help you avoid a number of disagreeable surprises.

Those stocks that track the market trend.

We have always been instructed to be unique and swim against the current. We've been told that champions don't follow the league; instead, they establish their own. In terms of the stock market, you wouldn't want to wager on such victors to begin with.

Such stocks can give you an outstanding start, but there is no way you can predict their performance. They are rugged and dangerous.

It is always preferable to invest in securities that trend with the market. This simply means to seek out equities that move in tandem with the market. If the market is favorable, these stocks will rise along with it. If market sentiment is pessimistic, they will demonstrate a downward trend. Such stocks will offer you the opportunity to profit during both bull and bear markets.

The majority of stable equities exhibit such fluctuations. These securities are dependable, and it is relatively simple to enter and exit a position on the same day. You would not want to invest in a stock that is rising while the market is falling, and as soon as you invest, the movement ceases or reverses. These securities are extremely hazardous, and there are many of them available. Keeping with the large and reputable companies can help you avoid such problems.

Good Fundamentals

Although many experts assert that fundamental analysis does not play a significant role in day trading, you should not blindly accept this assertion. When market sentiment is negative, only these types of equities survive. The reason is straightforward: when the tide recedes, traders prefer secure options.

Fundamentally sound stocks will always be more reliable and trustworthy. The market has confidence in them. Even minor news regarding their profits and expansion can cause large price movements in these equities. Even with major news, you may not see such movement in smaller equities because most traders do not trust them.

Initially, you should only invest in equities with solid fundamentals. They will help you comprehend how the market operates, and once you feel confident enough, you can begin experimenting with others.

Ownership Structure

This is yet another extremely vital factor that is typically overlooked. Institutional investors as well as retail investors and speculators like you and I own stocks. Both categories of investors have distinct purchasing and selling habits.

A retail investor may sell all of his or her shares at any time. When bad news arrives, retail investors are the first to abandon the market. Nevertheless, institutional investors cannot do so. They manage very extensive portfolios, and their decision-makers require sanction from multiple levels. This implies that a stock in which institutional investors have a significant stake will be more reliable, as it will continue to be volatile even after a major news event. The slow response of institutional investors ensures that there will be no sudden panic or crisis because a large number of equities are locked with them.

Understanding the risk associated with a stock can be facilitated by examining its ownership structure. If the majority of a stock's holders are retail investors, there is no way to know with certainty who they are. It is possible for a small group of individuals to generate artificial momentum in the stock market. They may also sell all their shares at once. Institutional investors are incapable of doing so.

As a novice trader, invest in equities in which institutional investors, such as mutual funds, hedge funds, etc., hold a substantial position. Such trading will limit your exposure to risk.

Understandable Chart Patterns

Once you begin perusing technical charts, you will discover that certain stocks make perfect sense. They adhere to patterns. Their actions are somewhat foreseeable. They are neither disjointed nor jerky. During this process, you will encounter equities that do not follow a pattern. They have no relationship with the indices or segments. They are wanderers. Such stocks are hazardous for day trading.

Every day trader must always keep in mind that they do not want to be trapped with a stock indefinitely. Regardless of how excellent or bad the stock is. You desire a swift entry and exit from this stock. The securities that do not adhere to a discernible pattern can become your responsibility. Once you acquire them, comprehending or predicting their behavior will become difficult, and you will be unable to escape.

The best solution is to seek out stocks with comprehensible chart patterns. The equities that move in a distinct pattern are always the best bets.

Adaptation to the New Flow

Lastly, sensitivity to the news flow can be a significant asset for intraday stocks. Some equities' responses to news events provide excellent trading opportunities. Nonetheless, some equities would remain stagnant regardless of the type of news that is released. They have a thick epidermis and become unpredictable in terms of commerce. You ought to avoid these securities.

Look for stocks that exhibit a high degree of volatility and sensitivity to news events, as well as trading opportunities.

High level

No matter how attractive the stock appears, if it lacks volume, it is unsuitable for intraday trading. These securities carry a very high risk of trapping you. This is the most important attribute to consider when selecting the stock of the day for trading.

Examining Levels of Support and Resistance

Consider investing in equities that are approaching their support or resistance levels. These securities may experience a breakout, and you will have an excellent opportunity to profit from them. Examine their levels thoroughly and investigate their historical trends. If they have done this in the past, it is a positive omen.

Near 52 Weeks Low or High Stocks that are near their 52-week low or high can also provide excellent trading opportunities. You can create a trading opportunity if you can correlate this with the fundamentals of these equities and if such traders can make a breakout and set new targets.

Winners and losers for the Week

These stocks will be in the news; consequently, trading in these stocks may be prudent. However, you must be cautious because a stock that has been gaining steadily for a while cannot continue to do so. As consolidation and profit booking can occur, you will need to assess whether the stock is already overbought or underbought. In addition to considering these factors, you should also consider whether the stock is undervalued or overvalued, as this will influence its rise and decline.

High Market Anticipation Stocks

These stocks would be following a wave, as they are newsmakers. Their movements are difficult to predict because market sentiments are more influential than fundamental and technical factors. These securities can also provide opportunities for short selling. However, you must remember that quick entry and exit from such equities is always optimal. You can become trapped if you attempt to maintain your position for too long, as they can take a sharp turn in any direction and seal you in.

From Your Specialty

Finally, select securities within your niche. As a novice trader, an open territory is always preferable. Nonetheless, as you progress in the stock market, you will realize that specializing is always the superior and more reliable option. Look for these characteristics in the securities from your field, and you will have few concerns.

www.ingramcontent.com/pod-product-compliance
Lightning Source LLC
Chambersburg PA
CBHW050235120526
44590CB00016B/2092